First Facts®

EXTREME PLANET

THE HIGHEST PLACES ON EARTH

by Martha E. H. Rustad

Consultant:
Niccole Villa Cerveny, PhD
Geography Faculty
Mesa Community College, Mesa, Arizona

CAPSTONE PRESS
a capstone imprint

First Facts is published by Capstone Press,
151 Good Counsel Drive, P.O. Box 669, Mankato, Minnesota 56002.
www.capstonepress.com

092009
005618CGS10

Books published by Capstone Press are manufactured with paper
containing at least 10 percent post-consumer waste.

Library of Congress Cataloging-in-Publication Data
Rustad, Martha E. H. (Martha Elizabeth Hillman), 1975–
    The highest places on Earth / by Martha E. H. Rustad.
        p. cm. — (First facts. Extreme planet)
    Includes bibliographical references and index.
    Summary: "An introduction to the highest places on earth, including maps and colorful photographs"
— Provided by publisher.
    ISBN 978-1-4296-3963-7 (library binding)
    1. Physical geography — Juvenile literature. 2. Altitudes — Juvenile literature. I. Title. II. Series.
GB58.R87 2010
910'.02143 — dc22   2009026038

Editorial credits
Erika L. Shores, editor; Ted Williams, designer, Svetlana Zhurkin, media researcher;
    Eric Manske, production specialist

Photo credits
Alamy/Panorama Media (Beijing), 10
Brian Grigsby, Education and Public Outreach Lead, Licancabur Expedition, 15
Getty Images/The Image Bank/Art Wolfe, cover, 19
Photodisc, 16
Photolibrary/Pawel Toczynski, 9
Shutterstock/enote, 13, Jeremy Richards, 15, my-summit, 21, rm, 7, yai112, 5

Essential content terms are **bold** and are defined at the bottom of the spread where they first appear.

TABLE OF CONTENTS

REACHING FOR THE SKY

Imagine standing on a mountain that is as high as airplanes fly. Temperatures are far below zero. You need layers of clothes to stay warm. The air is thin. You can hardly breathe.

Some places on earth have extreme **elevations**. Some spots tower more than 19,000 feet (5,800 meters) above sea level. Let's explore eight of the world's highest places.

elevation — the height above sea level; sea level is defined as zero elevation.

5

8 ANGEL FALLS

Angel Falls in Venezuela is the world's highest waterfall. It is 3,212 feet (979 meters) above sea level. The water falls more than a half-mile (0.8 kilometer). Wind turns much of the water into **mist** before it can hit the ground.

EXTREME FACT!

Water from the Caroní River rushes over a flat-topped mountain to make Angel Falls.

mist — a cloud of tiny water droplets in the air

ANGEL FALLS

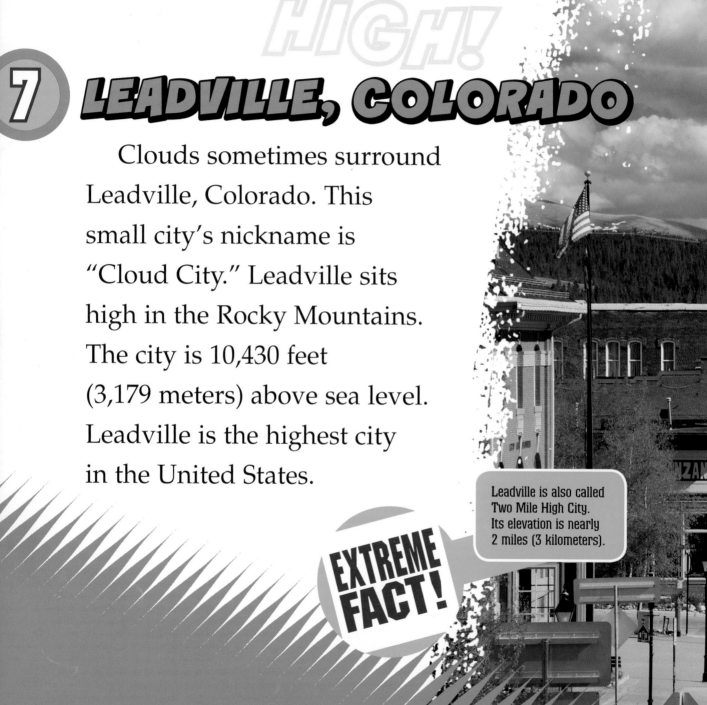

7 LEADVILLE, COLORADO

Clouds sometimes surround Leadville, Colorado. This small city's nickname is "Cloud City." Leadville sits high in the Rocky Mountains. The city is 10,430 feet (3,179 meters) above sea level. Leadville is the highest city in the United States.

EXTREME FACT!

Leadville is also called Two Mile High City. Its elevation is nearly 2 miles (3 kilometers).

LEADVILLE, COLORADO

WENQUAN, CHINA

N
W E
S

Wenquan is located near the Tanggula Mountains. These mountains reach heights of 20,000 feet (6,100 meters).

EXTREME FACT!

HIGH!

WENQUAN, CHINA 6

Travel to Wenquan and you'll feel like you're on top of the world. This village is located in the Tibet region of China. Wenquan sits at 16,730 feet (5,099 meters) above sea level. It's the world's highest place where people live.

HIGHER!

5 MOUNT KILIMANJARO

Africa's highest spot is in Tanzania. Mount Kilimanjaro stands 19,340 feet (5,895 meters) above sea level. Uhuru Peak is its highest part. The peak is so high that it's always covered in snow and ice.

peak — the pointed top of a mountain

As climbers move up Kilimanjaro, the temperature can drop by about 100 degrees.

EXTREME FACT!

MOUNT KILIMANJARO

13

4 LICANCÁBUR

On the border between Chile and Bolivia stands Licancábur volcano. Inside the volcano is the world's highest lake. The lake is 19,409 feet (5,916 meters) above sea level. Thousands of years ago, rainwater collected inside the volcano to form the lake.

EXTREME FACT!

Lake Titicaca is another high lake. It sits between Peru and Bolivia at 12,500 feet (3,810 meters) above sea level. It is the highest lake where boats can travel.

LICANCÁBUR VOLCANO

LAKE LICANCÁBUR

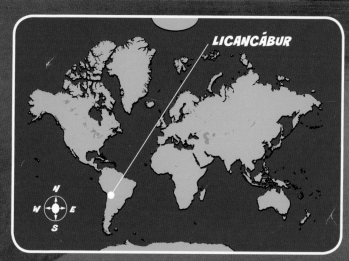

LICANCÁBUR

MOUNT MCKINLEY

W N E S

American Indians named Mount McKinley, "Denali." The name means "the high one."

EXTREME FACT!

MOUNT McKINLEY

Mount McKinley is 20,320 feet (6,194 meters) above sea level. North America's highest point is part of the Alaska Mountain Range. The weather is very cold on McKinley. Temperatures often drop to -50 degrees Fahrenheit (-46 degrees Celsius).

2

The world's second highest place is K2. This peak rises out of the Karakoram Mountain Range between Pakistan and China. It is 28,250 feet (8,611 meters) above sea level. K2 is steep and rocky. It's always covered in ice and snow.

EXTREME FACT!

Fewer than 300 climbers have ever reached the top of K2.

K2

1 MOUNT EVEREST

The world's highest place is in Asia's Himalaya Mountains. Mount Everest is 29,035 feet (8,850 meters) above sea level. About 4,000 people have climbed the towering mountain.

The world is full of high places. Which one would you like to visit?

EXTREME FACT!

Mount Everest is growing taller every year. Its height changes by a few inches each year.

MOUNT EVEREST

N
W E
S

GLOSSARY

elevation (el-uh-VAY-shuhn) — the height above sea level; sea level is defined as zero elevation.

mist (MIST) — a cloud of tiny water droplets in the air

peak (PEEK) — the pointed top of a mountain

sea level (SEE LEV-uhl) — the average level of the ocean's surface; sea level is a starting point from which to measure height or depth.

volcano (vol-KAY-noh) — a mountain with vents through which lava, ash, and gas erupt

READ MORE

Green, Jen. *Mountains around the World.* Geography Now. New York: PowerKids Press, 2009.

Heinrichs, Ann. *Mount Everest.* Nature's Wonders. New York: Marshall Cavendish Benchmark, 2009.

Hurley, Michael. *The World's Most Amazing Mountains.* Landform Top Tens. Chicago: Raintree, 2009.

Watson, Galadriel. *Angel Falls: The Highest Waterfall in the World.* Natural Wonders. New York: Weigl Publishers, 2005.

INTERNET SITES

FactHound offers a safe, fun way to find Internet sites related to this book. All of the sites on FactHound have been researched by our staff.

Here's all you do:

Visit *www.facthound.com*

FactHound will fetch the best sites for you!

INDEX